The
ULTIMATE
Guide to
TEAM BUILDING

Casey Johnson

To order additional copies of this book, contact:
Xlibris Corporation
1-888-795-4274
www.Xlibris.com
Orders@Xlibris.com

TABLE OF CONTENTS

I. INTRODUCTION

What is a team? Well, that definition is really up to the one asking the question. Depending on the outcome that you are trying to achieve, team can have different meanings. In general, a team is a group of individuals established together to achieve a common goal or objective. Teams are a very important part of today's society. Whether it is a SWAT team designed to minimize the risk to potential bystanders, or an Engineering team working to design the next fighter aircraft, each team's success depends on the formation of that team. We have all been a part of a situation where you were placed on a team that was doomed to fail. What about when you were in school and teams were decided by drawing numbers out of a hat? What if that technique was used nationally in organizations today? Would we be as technologically advanced as we are today? I'm pretty sure the consensus is that we would be a total mess given that this philosophy was the common approach to team formulation in our society. Building a team is a very critical tool that a leader needs in his or her tool chest, but often this quality is overlooked. You must have a keen ability to determine projects needs in order to pin point the dynamics that a team requires. As a leader, you must be able to do all of the following:

1. Define the project

2. Set the project goals

3. Define the type of team necessary to complete the project

4. Set the team milestones needed to reach the end goals

5. Choose a diversified and dynamic team by correlating project goals with peoples' skills

6. Strategically integrate the team to stimulate the value added assets of each member

7. Wait for results (Have faith in your ability to perform the top 6 items successfully), and

8. Supervise when necessary.

This guide should serve as a tool to help you maximize the success of the teams you form, and to accomplish all of the fore mentioned tasks. In the next section, you will see the rationalization behind these eight simple revolving steps.

Together Everyone Achieves More

II. EIGHT REVOLVING STEPS

I have suggested the eight steps in this guide based on an extensive amount of research and practical real life experience. I have collaborated and simplified the steps of many highly respected management techniques in order to create this leadership guide. These eight steps are building blocks dependent on each other, and I firmly believe following them will dramatically increase a leaders potential to truly develop and establish an effective team within their organization. The eight steps should be used as a repeating cycle based on each new project a leader is presented with. The eight steps included in this guide are as follows:

1. Define the Project

2. Set the Project Goals

3. Define the Team

4. Set the Team Goals

5. Choose the Team

6. Integrate the Team

7. Wait, and last but certainly not least

8. Supervise

The following chart depicts a more visual aid of the eight step cycle.

EIGHT REVOLVING STEPS:

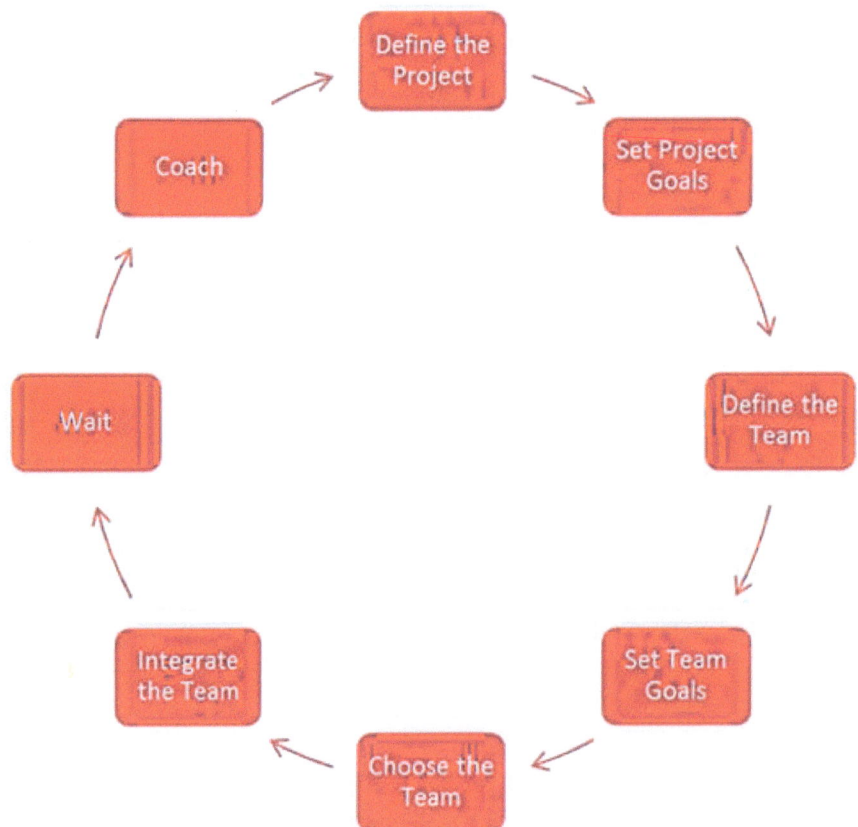

III. DEFINE THE PROJECT

This is the first step that will help you determine the characteristics needed for your team. First, there has to be a need for a team. Whether it is a problem that needs resolution or a design that needs formulation, both require a talented and diverse team of individuals in order to solve. This phase simply defines why you are seeking to form a team. Once this is known, then you need to outline the details of the project to follow. Below are some questions that can routinely be answered in order to help you complete this step of the cycle.

- What am I trying to accomplish?

- What will be required to accomplish this task?

- How long will it take to accomplish this task?

- What is the desired outcome of this task?

Once you have answered these four questions, then you should have a better understanding of what you are trying to accomplish with the team. These questions should give you a good descriptive definition of the scope and purpose of the project. Now that you have defined your project at hand, it is time to set the project goals!

Hint: Keep the project definition developed in this phase to revert back to when needed.

This Phase Gets the Gears Spinning!!!

<u>Practical Example:</u> At a former employer, I facilitated a team of quick response "Enhanced Planners". Our job was to dive deep into a troublesome process, and improve it in any way possible. Ultimately, we were tasked to eliminate waste; resulting in time savings, reduced cost, and reduced effort to complete the task. This included placing visual aids into the routings generated by planning, exploring point of use tooling, and many other possible alternatives to the norm. However, in order to truly improve the process in the quick window of opportunity we were allotted, it required us to first define what the troublesome area actually was, in other words "defining the project". Was it the structure modifications that needed these enhancements? Was it tooling modifications? Was it simply physical limitations that created the troublesome process? These are all questions that we had to answer in order to tactfully and efficiently attack the troublesome areas without having to go through a complete process audit. Given our unique situation, complete process observations weren't always possible. Therefore, we had to place precise consideration on defining the project in order to make any impact. Otherwise our effort was wasted on something that did not produce much value for the company.

IV. SET PROJECT GOALS

In the previous phase, you defined the project. In doing so, you developed requirements that needed to be met before the completion of the project could occur. In this phase, you will set the project goals needed to reach the completion of the project. These goals should directly align with your project requirements, but with time constraints added to them. Consider this phase more like setting project milestones. Project milestones should be obtainable and realistic to prevent project failure. Remember, meeting these milestones ensures overall project success. Also, in forming these goals, you need to ensure that they are understandable. Everyone involved has to be able to comprehend the project goals without having to seek additional clarification. This will prevent the loss of time during the lifecycle of your project. Some things to keep in mind during this phase include:

- Ensure goals / milestones you set are obtainable and realistic.

- Ensure goals / milestones reflect proper time frames needed to meet time constraints of the overall project.

- Ensure goals / milestones are understandable to everyone impacted by the project.

Practical Example: Working off the previous example, once we defined what exactly needed to be improved in the process, we then set project goals in order to accomplish all the enhancements necessary within the time constraints. These served as our roadmap to project success.

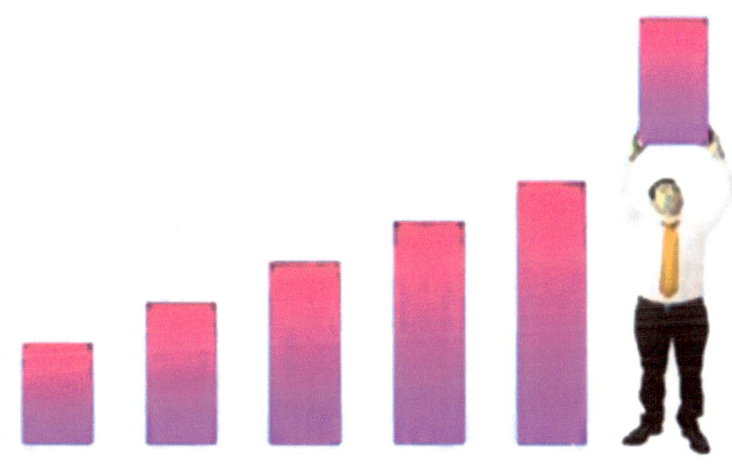

Don't Set Your Goals TOO HIGH !!!

V. DEFINE THE TEAM

The next step in the cycle is to define the team. This step very closely resembles the steps taken when defining the project. The difference is that, now you are defining the team that will best fit the characteristics of the project. Once you have defined the project and set the project goals, then this step should be a breeze. All you have to do is define the skills, traits, and characteristics that you need on your team in order to fulfill the project requirements. When defining your team, you need to ensure that you examine all aspects of the project. For example, if your project involves intense electrical wiring, then your team should include a skilled electrician as a necessity. It really is that simple. Also, when defining your team you must take into consideration what level of experience the project actually requires. Do you need a group of veterans that know the ins and outs of the scope of the project, or does the project have some good developmental characteristics for your younger generation? Possibly, a mixture of both would fit this project best. This step can be summarized in a few questions below to ease you through this process:

- What type of skill set will this project entail?
- What is the difficulty level of this project?
- Can associates be used for this project or will it require veteran skills?
- Can this project entail only company people or will alternate sources be needed?

Answering these four simple questions should provide you with an excellent starting point when defining your team. This could be a very crucial step in determining the quality of your project outcome.

Practical Example: At a former corporation, I facilitated a team that had determined there was a huge bottleneck in one of the aircraft electrical installations. We took the initiative to tackle this bottleneck, and sought to eliminate it from being a burden in the future. This particular installation was drastically impacting the schedule of other dependent installations. Long story short, this installation was costing the company money due to its inefficiency. However, our team did not consist of any electrical experience, and the study of the installation drawing would have taken far too long due to its complexity. Our solution, as a team, was to temporarily bring in an electrical planner for the duration of this process. This is a perfect example of defining your team and the capabilities needed to reach its ultimate ability.

What tools will it require to complete the task?

VI. SET TEAM GOALS

After you have defined the team, it is time to set the team goals. Again, this process should closely resemble that of the project goals, only now directed at the team specifically. In this step, a flowchart can be a very useful tool to provide somewhat of a direction for the team. There should be specific milestones set for the team in order to accomplish the project in the allotted amount of time. You should also ensure that the team goals cooperate with the project requirements. For instance, if certain tasks need to be accomplished before other task can be started, then that priority should be established within the team goals set in this stage. In other words, these task goals should precede future task goals to ensure your project stays on track. Another very useful tool in helping define the teams' goals is the Critical Path Method (See Appendix). This method will mathematically determine in what order task should be accomplished. In this step, you can simply align the team goals with the critical path. This will ensure that you will be successful. Below, I have shown a very basic example of a critical path network. Critical paths can sometimes be much more involved and complex than the example shown here.

Critical Path Example:

Critical Path →(Blue)

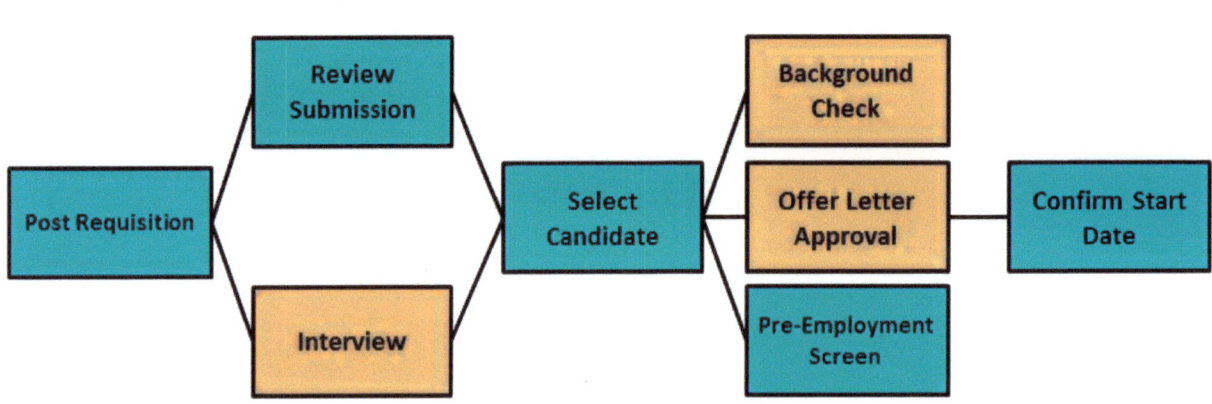

Practical Example: Working off the previous example, even though we brought in an electrical planner to aid us in the study of the bottleneck installation, we still needed to set team goals. Due to the lack of electrical experience on our team, we had to implement these team goals in order to utilize the electrical planning resource to the utmost capacity. For instance, we had a team member that was extremely efficient at creating work order routings. Therefore, we set goals for this individual to do such efforts on the electrical planner's behalf, in order to optimize the electrical experience in other areas of the project. Setting goals for team and the team members proved to be a very vital step in getting this process improvement initiative out on time.

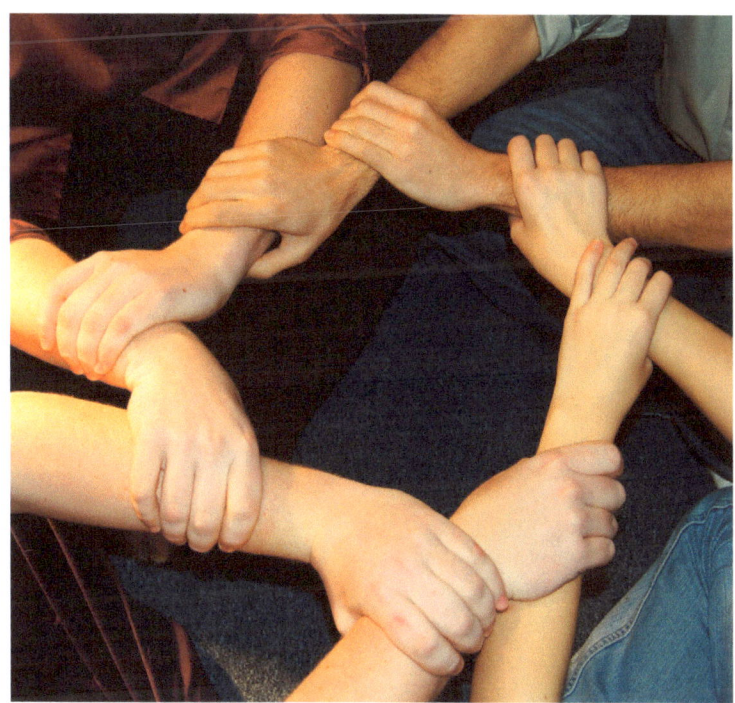

Plan the Path to Success!!!

VII. CHOOSE THE TEAM

The next step in the cycle is to choose the team. In this step, you will simply target the individuals with the skill sets that you defined in the "Define the Team" step of the cycle. When you defined the team, you came up with skill set and variations of characteristics that will be needed to complete this project. In this step, you will simply select the individuals that fit each scenario the best. There are several things to consider when choosing the team. You need to ensure the level of knowledge of the individuals chosen matches the level of difficulty that the project entails. This can sometimes be a complicated task. Sound judgment plays a key role in this step. Another consideration when choosing your team, is to ensure that the individuals chosen can set aside adequate time in their day to effectively contribute to the project. If you choose someone that has too many irons in the fire, then they may cause a delay in the timeline of your project. For the most part, this should be a fairly simple step, since everything has already been previously defined.

<u>Practical Example:</u> Although we already had a set team of enhanced planners in the previous examples, the projects still required special attention from skilled individuals. Bringing in an electrical planner with the background to do the electrical installation study is an example of needing a certain skillset. Every enhancement that a team makes will inevitably require effort from outside resources. We, as a team, must choose outside resources wisely, and ensure company time and resources are not wasted.

Choose Your Team Wisely!!!

VIII. INTEGRATE THE TEAM

The next step in the cycle is to integrate the team. In this step, you want to combine the skills and talents of your team effectively. Consider it like piecing together a puzzle. No one piece fits in multiple spots. In a puzzle, you must find the spot that the piece fits, and place it in that spot to complete the puzzle. Integrating your team is no different from completing the puzzle. Each person or skill set fits best with certain other people or skill sets. For example, if your project was to build a house, then you would have all kinds of skill sets. Integrating your painter with your plumber would not be a very good combination. They are two totally different skill sets, and occur at totally different times during the completion of the house. On the other hand, if you integrated the plumber and the carpenter, then this would be a better combination. They may be different skill sets, but they have a need to work together. The carpenter has to know where to stud around the plumbing, and the plumber needs to know the lay out of the walls to rough in the plumbing. Although your project may not entail building a house, relationships such as these will exists within your team. It will be crucial for you to appropriately identify these relationships and integrate them in this step of the cycle. This step, if done correctly, will ensure a smooth road to completion.

Practical Example: Again, referring to the enhanced planning team mentioned in previous examples, we had a budget that had to be met with each project selection. We had to provide metrics on the actuals that accumulated from our enhancements. At any time, our jobs could be eliminated if they proved to be unbeneficial for the company. To ensure that this did not happen, team integration played an astronomical part. With each improvement initiative we divvied up the work load, and set integration points. Integration points were where work from the team would come together in stages to output a final product. You can see where careful communication and availability is a necessity for proper integration to occur. Each team member must coordinate with one another to know exactly where his or her process starts and stops. This ensures that the integration of project milestones leads to a smooth transition into project completion.

People + Skills = Puzzle Pieces to a Successful Team

IX. WAIT

Wait? Where does that fit into the picture? No mistake, this is a key step to the effective building of a project team. Let's pause, and take a step back for a minute. So far we have defined the project, set the project goals, defined the team, set the team goals, chosen the team, and integrated the team. By this step, your team has been established, and you have integrated them into proper working relationships. This step is simply a reminder, to sit back and let your team perform. If you followed the steps correctly, then your team has no choice but to accomplish the tasks successfully. You have given the team the goals of the project, and you have put time and thought into the individuals that you have selected. Therefore, if your judgment plays out right, then essentially your job is complete. However, we know that this is not a perfect world, and complications will arise. Isn't it Murphy's Law that states, "Anything that can go wrong, will go wrong"? That is the reason that we must address the next and final step in the cycle, supervise.

WAIT.......Monitor Your Teams Performance!!!

X. SUPERVISE

The final step in the cycle is to supervise your team. Although you have spent the effort and the time creating a very reliable team, they will need help along the way. Sometimes people get wrapped up in the task at hand and often veer off the beaten path. It is your job, as a leader, to simply keep them on the right path. If you have followed this cycle effectively, then this is all the supervision your team will likely need. Just watch them perform and keep them on the track of success. You may also need to provide them with resources that are not readily available. The one thing to remember as you supervise is not to get in the way of your team. Supervising, in this instance is simply coaching, not intervening or directing. Your team should have the talent and skills to complete the tasks required for the project, let them utilize them. Often supervisor forget this, and try to become micromanagers. This creates a bad environment for your team, and often leads to failure. Be sure to stay out of there way, and let them show you what they can do. Key points to take away from this step are:

- Don't micromanage your team!

- Provide them with the resources that they need, when they need it!

- Keep them from getting off track!

<u>Practical Example:</u> In previous examples, this falls directly in the hands of the enhanced planning team leader. The leader did a fantastic job of not directing, but rather coaching. He sit back and truly waited on the team to perform. He was there to refocus the team on project/team goals in the event the team got off track, but otherwise he stood clear and allowed his team to do what they do best.

Don't Micromanage Your Team!!!
Trust Your Formulation!!!
Provide Them With the Necessary Resources!!!
Keep Them From Getting Off Track!!!

XI. CONCLUSION

The ability to effectively build project teams is critical to project success. The steps in this guide will drastically increase your potential to effectively build these project teams on a repetitive basis. No step in this cycle is more important than another, and they all play a key role in developing successful teams. I developed this guide based on past military experience in team formulation, current team involvement, and experience in the facilitation of all kind of project teams. I feel this guide can be used across many fields and concentrations. I strongly believe that the key to successful development of project teams lies within the steps of this guide. I encourage every supervisor at every level to give this guide the opportunity to provide them with team building success.

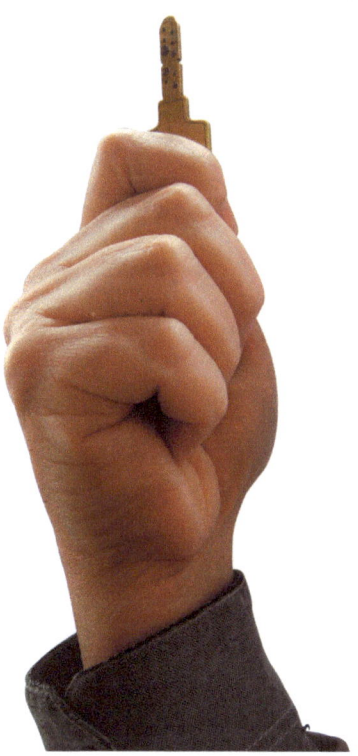

XII. APPENDIX

Critical Path Method (CPM)

- CPM provides the following benefits:

- A graphical view of the project

- Prediction of the time required to complete the project

- Shows which activities are critical to maintain the project schedule

CPM models activities and events of a project as a network. Activities are depicted as nodes on the network, and events that signify the beginning or ending of activities are depicted as arcs or lines between the nodes.

The following is an example of a CPM diagram:

Critical Path →(Green)

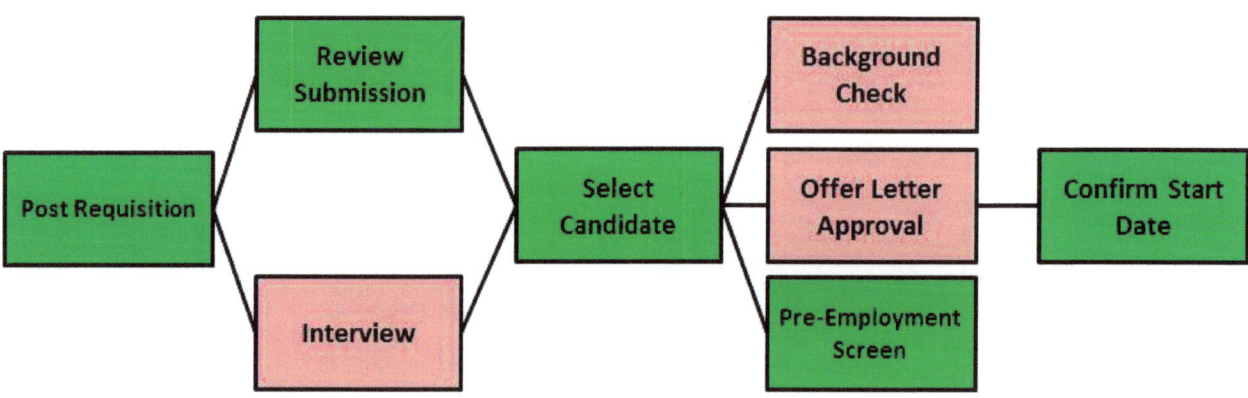

Steps in CPM Project Planning include:

1. Specify the individual activities that will be involved

2. Determine the sequence in which those activities should occur

3. Draw a network diagram of those activities

4. Estimate the completion time required for each activity

5. Identify the Critical Path (The longest path through the network)

6. Update the CPM diagram as the project progresses

XIII. REFERENCES

1. Dorf, Richard C. (1999). <u>The Technology: Management Handbook</u>. Florida: CRC Press LLC.

2. Hans, Thamhain (2005). <u>Management of Technology: Managing Effectively in Technology-Intensive Organizations</u>. New Jersey: John Wiley & Son's, Inc.

3. Kerzner, Harold, (2004). <u>Advanced Project Management: Best Practices on Implementation</u>. New Jersey: John Wiley & Son's, Inc.

4. Meier, Steven R. (2008). "Building and Managing an Effective Project Team." *Defense AT&L*, September – October, 2008

5. NetMBA.com. (2002), CPM – Critical Path Method. Retrieved February 01, 2010 from http://www.netmba.com/operations/project/cpm/

6. Wallace, Simon. (1999), Team Building, Collaboration, and Communication. Retrieved March 15, 2010 from http://www.epmbook.com/team.htm

ABOUT THE AUTHOR

My name is Casey Johnson. I went into the United States Air Force at the age of 18, and spent 4 years of my early life overseas. During my tenure, I specialized in the production, assembly, testing, storage, transportation, and loading of conventional and non-conventional weapons. I rapidly progressed through the ranks during those 4 years, reaching a SSgt. supervisory level for the final 8 months of my Air Force career. I grew immensely as a traditional mass production assembly line supervisor at a very young age. This experience intrigued me and sparked the passion I would soon acquire for operations, manufacturing, and the continuous improvement process. Upon completion of my 4 year enlistment, I wanted to build upon my on hand experience with technical knowledge. I enrolled in the Industrial Engineering program at a branch of Texas A&M University immediately upon my separation from the USAF. After successful completion of the undergraduate program, I decided to carry on my educational journey. I later received a graduate degree in management with a focus on operations and technology. After completing my education accomplishments, I began to add to the experience I acquired in the USAF. I have spent time at companies such as; Lockheed Martin, L-3 Communications, and Flowserve.

On a personal note, growing up I was blessed with the most inspirational set of parents a boy could ever ask for. My mother, Nita, has inspired me by her strength to overcome some of the burdens placed on her from an unfortunate accident at an early age. My father, Dennis, has motivated me to be the man I have become. His dedication and will to succeed from practically nothing is unsurpassable. Also, I have been blessed with an amazing wife, Ashley. She has answered all my prayers following a tragic divorce. Ashley has opened my eyes to a new life. She has reenergized my passion and fire for Christ, my lord and savior. God's plan has been apparent in my life, and I have no regrets. Through my divorce, I was left with the most amazing gift from god, my 4 year old daughter, Jaylie. She was my strength to make it through, and remains the light in my life and the pulse in my heart. I cannot imagine life without her. Alongside her, I now have the luxury of raising a beautiful step daughter, Anabell. She captured a piece of my heart from the beginning, and has taught me how to love something that is not rightfully your own. We are surrounded by an amazing extended family, and I could not be more thankful for where God has placed me in his world. I now know through all of my experience, that God has a plan for each of our lives and if you look to him through the valleys and atop the mountains you will be blessed.

Casey Johnson
B.S. of Industrial Engineering
M. S. of Technology and Operations Management
Lean Practitioner / Six Sigma Black Belt
(903) 715-0286 or cfjohnson1985@gmail.com